NEON RECKONING: SHADOWS OF TRUTH

Roman Bonari

CONTENTS

Table of Contents

CHAPTER 1

Neon Beginnings

The city skyline was an enigma of light and shadow, a canvas where neon signs and holographic billboards danced in an endless loop of vibrant colors. Amidst this technicolor dreamscape, Cray stood on a high vantage point, his silhouette etched against the pulsating lights of the metropolis. His hands were buried in the pockets of his weathered jeans, and his ginger hair, unkempt yet striking, was a stark contrast against the myriad of hues reflecting off the glass and steel around him. His green eyes, betraying a wisdom and depth beyond his 17 years, scanned the horizon, observing the sprawling urban expanse with a mixture of awe and cynicism.

Below, the city thrummed with life; flying cars zipped between towering skyscrapers, their trails of light weaving a dynamic tapestry in the night sky. The streets, a labyrinth of neon and noise, were teeming with people from all walks of life. Street vendors hawked their wares with boisterous energy, their voices mingling with the eclectic sounds of the city. In the distance, the faint hum of machinery and the rhythmic beat of electronic music provided a backdrop to the urban symphony.

To his left, absorbed in her own world, was Eloise. Her focus was unyielding as her fingers danced over a swarm of nanobots, each tiny machine a glowing speck in the dim light of their hideout. Eloise's workspace was a chaotic tapestry of creation, with husks of discarded tech and half-assembled gadgets forming a peculiar mosaic on the ground around her. Her dark hair was pulled back into a messy bun, strands escaping to frame her concentrated face. The light from the tiny screens in front of her cast an ethereal glow on her features, highlighting her intense, dark eyes that rarely strayed from her work.

Cray watched her for a moment, marveling at her absolute dedication. Eloise was a genius in the realm of micro-technology, and her work with nanobots was nothing short of revolutionary. The tiny machines were her soldiers, responding to her every command with precision and agility. They were currently assembling what appeared to be a compact, yet intricate, piece of technology, the purpose of which was known only to her.

Breaking the silence, Cray called out, "Eloise, how's it looking on your end?"

Without looking up, Eloise replied, "Almost there. These nanobots are going to change the game. Just you wait, Cray."

Cray smiled slightly, his gaze returning to the city. This place, with all its contradictions and challenges, was their playground and battlefield. It was a world of immense beauty and rampant corruption, a place where the bright lights often cast the darkest shadows. And it was up to them, a small group of rebels and geniuses, to uncover the truths hidden within this dazzling facade.

As he stood there, the city's vibrant energy seemed to pulse through him, a reminder of the mission that lay ahead. They were the unseen, the underestimated, working in the shadows of this neon-drenched world. And they were just getting started. Eloise finally looked up, her eyes meeting Cray's. "You're still dreaming about the stars, aren't you?" she asked, a playful yet knowing tone in her voice. Cray's fascination with the night sky was well-known to her; it was a rare glimpse into the softer side of a young man who often seemed too tough for his age.

"Maybe," Cray responded, his eyes not leaving the cityscape. "Or maybe I'm just looking for a sign."

Eloise chuckled and turned back to her work. "Well, if you find one, let me know."

The gentle banter faded into the background as Cray's thoughts wandered. This city, for all its technological marvels, held a dark underbelly. As a skilled hacker, Cray had seen enough to know that beneath the neon facade lay a web of corruption and deceit. It was a world where information was the most valuable commodity, and those who controlled it held the power.

As if on cue, a series of faint beeps emanated from a device on Cray's wrist. He glanced at the screen, which displayed a string of coded messages. "Looks like we've got something," he muttered, decrypting the data with a few swift taps.

"What is it?" Eloise asked, her attention now fully on Cray.

"An anomaly in the city's surveillance network. There's a blind spot, and it's moving."

"A moving blind spot? That's new," Eloise mused, her curiosity piqued. "Do you think it's them?"

"It's possible," Cray said, his expression turning serious. "If it is, we need to find out why. A blind spot in the surveillance could mean someone is trying to hide something big. Something worth hiding from the all-seeing eyes of the city."

Eloise nodded in agreement, her mind already racing with possibilities. The city's surveillance system was notoriously omnipresent, making any sort of anomaly worth investigating. It could be a glitch, but in their line of work, they couldn't afford to assume anything.

"Let's gear up," Cray said decisively. "If there's a secret lurking in this city, we're going to uncover it."

The two of them moved into action, preparing their equipment with practiced efficiency. Eloise gathered her nanobots, now programmed for reconnaissance, and loaded them into a sleek, metallic container. Cray, on the other hand, equipped himself with a portable hacking device, its screen flickering to life with complex algorithms and codes.

As they geared up, the dynamic between them was palpable; they were a team in every sense of the word, their skills complementing each other's perfectly. Eloise, with her groundbreaking work in nanotechnology, provided the eyes and ears, while Cray, a prodigy in the dark arts of hacking, navigated the digital labyrinth of the city's networks.

"Remember, we need to be careful," Cray reminded Eloise as they prepared to leave their hideout. "Whoever created this blind spot knows what they're doing. This isn't amateur hour."

Eloise gave a confident nod. "Don't worry, I've updated the nanobots with the latest stealth tech. They won't be detected."

With a final check of their gear, they stepped out into the night. The city, alive with its nocturnal heartbeat, seemed oblivious to the two figures moving stealthily through its veins. Cray and Eloise blended into the shadows, making their way towards the location of the mysterious blind spot.

As they navigated the maze of streets, the city's true face began to reveal itself. Beneath the neon glamor, there was a grittiness, a raw edge that spoke of the struggles and conflicts within. The alleys were lined with remnants of a day's hustle - abandoned tech, graffiti screaming silent protests, and the occasional weary soul seeking refuge in the darkness.

Reaching the designated area, they paused, taking in the surroundings. The blind spot was located in one of the less affluent parts of the city, a stark contrast to the glitzy downtown areas. Buildings here were older, their once-bright facades now dulled and weathered. The air was thick with the scent of rust and unfulfilled dreams.

"This is it," Cray whispered, activating his device. The screen displayed a real-time map, a blinking dot indicating their location right in the heart of the anomaly.

Eloise released a handful of nanobots, which buzzed to life and dispersed into the night, invisible to the naked eye. They would scout the area, feeding information back to her handheld monitor.

As they waited in silence, the city around them seemed to hold its breath, the usual cacophony dimming to a hushed whisper. They were on the brink of uncovering something, standing at the edge of a revelation that could shake the very foundations of their neon-drenched world. The city night whispered around them as Cray and Eloise waited in tense silence. The nanobots, now mere specks in the vast urban landscape, methodically scanned the area, their findings streaming live to Eloise's monitor. The data, a cryptic ballet of numbers and symbols, flickered rapidly on the screen.

Suddenly, Eloise's eyes narrowed. "Cray, look at this," she said, her voice a mix of excitement and disbelief. The data on the screen had revealed something unexpected – a hidden network, intricate and well-disguised, operating right under the city's nose.

Cray leaned in, his eyes quickly decoding the information. "This... this is big," he murmured. "It looks like an underground network, completely off the grid. And it's right here, in this sector."

The revelation sent a ripple of adrenaline through them. An underground network, hidden from the city's all-seeing eyes, could mean a multitude of things - none of them insignificant. It could be a haven for the city's rebels, a secret hub for illicit activities, or something entirely unknown, waiting to be uncovered.

"We need to investigate this," Eloise said, determination etched in her tone. "If we can tap into this network, we might uncover what they're hiding."

Cray nodded, his mind already racing with possibilities. "Let's do it. But we have to be careful. Whoever set this up knows what they're doing. We're stepping into unknown territory."

With a plan forming, they began their careful descent into the heart of the anomaly. The city around them felt different now, charged with the potential of their discovery. The neon lights seemed to blaze a little brighter, casting long shadows on their path.

As they moved forward, the chapter closed on their first step into a deeper mystery, one that promised to reveal the hidden truths of their neon-drenched world.

End of Chapter 1

CHAPTER 2

The Hidden Network

The night was deepening, casting its veil over the city as Cray and Eloise navigated the labyrinthine streets towards the heart of the anomaly. The air was charged with an electric current of anticipation, each step taking them closer to the unknown.

As they approached the coordinates pinpointed by the nanobots, the neighborhood transformed. The bright neon lights of the city center gave way to dimly lit streets, where shadows played tricks on the eye, and every footstep echoed with a sense of foreboding.

"There," Eloise whispered, pointing to a nondescript building nestled between two larger structures. Its facade was unremarkable, but the data didn't lie – this was the location of the hidden network's signal.

Cray's fingers flew over his device, attempting to breach the building's security. The task was formidable; whoever had set up this network was a master of their craft. After several tense minutes, a soft beep signaled success. They exchanged a look of triumph and cautiously entered the building.

Inside, the air was stale, the silence a stark contrast to the constant hum of the city. The hallway was lined with doors, each as unassuming as the next. They needed more information, a way to determine where this network was hidden.

As they advanced, a sudden noise stopped them in their tracks.

From one of the rooms, the sound of hushed voices seeped out. Eloise motioned to Cray, and they approached the door, listening intently.

The conversation inside was cryptic, mentions of data caches and security protocols. Cray and Eloise exchanged a glance; this was it. But before they could act, the door swung open, revealing a figure that neither of them had expected.

Standing before them was not an adversary, but Kai, a former classmate known for his exceptional skills in cyber engineering. His appearance was disheveled, his eyes wide with a mix of surprise and fear.

"Kai?" Eloise uttered in disbelief.

"Cray, Eloise, what are you doing here?" Kai's voice was a mix of astonishment and apprehension.

"We could ask you the same," Cray replied, his mind racing. Kai's presence here changed everything. Was he part of the network, or like them, just trying to uncover its secrets?

Kai hesitated, then beckoned them inside. "I'm not your enemy," he said quickly. "But we need to talk. It's about the network."

As they stepped into the room, the chapter closed, leaving a trail of questions. Kai's involvement, the purpose of the hidden network, and how it all connected to the larger secrets of the city remained shrouded in mystery.

Kai's room was a cluttered haven of technology, with screens displaying streams of data and walls lined with complex circuitry. The dim light from the monitors cast a glow on his anxious face as he closed the door behind them.

"Cray, Eloise, I didn't expect to find anyone else here, especially not you two," Kai started, his voice a mix of nervousness and urgency. "This network... it's not what you think. It's part of something much bigger, more dangerous."

Eloise's brows furrowed in concern. "What do you mean? We thought it was just a hidden data hub."

Kai shook his head, pacing the room. "It's a node, yes, but it's part of a decentralized network. And it's not just about data storage or illicit deals. It's a part of a resistance movement, against the corporations controlling the city."

Cray and Eloise exchanged a glance, the gravity of Kai's revelation sinking in. The idea of a resistance movement changed the narrative entirely. It wasn't just a matter of uncovering corporate secrets anymore; it was about the struggle for power in the city.

"But why are you involved, Kai?" Cray asked, suspicion lacing his tone. "How do we know we can trust you?"

Kai stopped, meeting Cray's gaze. "Because I'm one of the architects of this network. I helped build it, not for profit or power, but to fight against the corporate stranglehold on our city. And I need your help."

Eloise stepped forward. "What kind of help?"

Before Kai could answer, the room's monitors flickered, and a siren blared outside. Red and blue lights flashed through the window, casting an ominous glow.

"They've found us," Kai said, his voice tense. "The network's been compromised, and they've traced it here."

Cray and Eloise's hearts raced. The situation had escalated beyond their initial plan. They were now in the midst of a conflict that threatened to engulf the entire city.

"We need to leave, now," Cray said, his decision firm. "But this isn't over. We're going to find out what's really going on, and we're going to end it."

The three of them quickly gathered the essential gear, wiping Kai's systems to leave no trace behind. As they slipped out the back door into the maze of dark alleys, the chapter closed, leaving a trail of unanswered questions and a city on the brink of a revelation that could shake its very foundations.

As they navigate the dark alleys, evading the approaching sirens, Cray, Eloise, and now Kai, must come to terms with the larger conflict they have become part of. The next chapter should open with them planning their next move, while a mysterious figure watches them from the shadows, hinting at a new player in the game or a potential ally or enemy. This unseen observer sets the stage for further intrigue and deepens the mystery of the resistance movement.

End of Chapter 2

CHAPTER 3

Shadows and Alliances

The night was a blanket of secrecy as Cray, Eloise, and Kai navigated the labyrinthine alleys, the sound of sirens fading behind them. The adrenaline of the escape pulsed through their veins, mingling with a torrent of questions about the resistance movement and their role in it.

As they reached the relative safety of a deserted underpass, Kai led them to a hidden alcove, barely visible in the dim light. "We can talk here," he said, his voice still tinged with urgency.

Eloise, catching her breath, turned to Kai. "You need to start talking, fast. What is this resistance movement? And why are the authorities after it?"

Kai's eyes were a mixture of fear and resolve. "The movement is called 'The Shadow Network.' It started as a small group of techies and hackers fighting against corporate control, but it's grown. We're not just a thorn in their side anymore; we're a threat."

Cray, leaning against the cold wall, processed this information. "So, you're telling us that by tapping into the network, we've put ourselves in the crosshairs?"

Kai nodded solemnly. "Yes, but it's more than that. The Shadow Network has information, evidence of corporate corruption and exploitation that could upend the city. That's why they're hunting us."

Before they could delve deeper into the conversation, a shadow detached itself from the darkness of the underpass. A figure stepped into the faint light, their features obscured by a hood.

"Kai," the figure spoke, their voice low and controlled. "I see you've brought friends."

Kai stiffened, recognition dawning on his face. "Rynn," he acknowledged. "They're with me. They can be trusted."

Rynn, the mysterious figure, shifted their gaze to Cray and Eloise. "Trust is a rare commodity these days," they said, appraising them. "Especially in our line of work."

Eloise met Rynn's gaze, her own determination unwavering. "We want the same thing you do. To expose the truth."

Rynn considered her words, then nodded slowly. "Very well. But know this; you're deeper in this than you realize. The Shadow Network isn't just fighting the corporations. We're fighting for the soul of the city."

The weight of Rynn's words hung in the air, solidifying the gravity of their situation. They were no longer just rebels seeking the truth; they were part of a larger battle, one that encompassed the very essence of their city.

As they gathered around Rynn, ready to plan their next move, the chapter closed, leaving a sense of foreboding and anticipation for the challenges ahead.

Gathered in the dim underpass, the group formed a circle of wary yet determined faces. Rynn, the enigmatic figure who had emerged from the shadows, seemed to carry an air of authority and insight. Their gaze lingered on each member of the group, assessing their resolve.

"You need to understand the stakes," Rynn began, their voice echoing slightly in the concrete space. "The Shadow Network has been infiltrating and gathering data on the corporations for months. We're close to exposing their deepest secrets, but with the network compromised, we're all in danger."

Eloise, her mind racing with the implications, spoke up. "So, what's the plan? How do we get this information out before they shut us down?"

Rynn pulled out a small, encrypted data drive. "This contains coordinates to a secure location where the network's data is backed up. But it's heavily guarded, both physically and digitally. Retrieving it won't be easy."

Cray stepped forward, his expression resolute. "We'll do it. We have the skills needed to pull this off. But we'll need your help, Rynn. You know the network better than anyone."

Rynn nodded, a flicker of approval in their eyes. "I'll provide you with the schematics and cover your digital tracks. But once you're in, you'll be on your own."

Kai, who had been silent, finally spoke. "I'll help with the tech side. I have access to tools that can aid us in bypassing security."

The group formed a plan, each member contributing their expertise. They would infiltrate the secure location, retrieve the data, and expose the corporations' corruption to the world. It was a daunting task, fraught with risk, but they were united in their cause.

As they finalized their strategy, a sudden disruption shattered the silence of the night. The distant sound of sirens began to approach again, this time accompanied by the unmistakable hum of drone surveillance.

"They're closing in on us," Rynn said, urgency lacing their voice. "We need to move, now."

The group quickly dispersed, melting into the shadows of the city. As they split up to avoid detection, the chapter closed, leaving a trail of tension and uncertainty. The stakes had been raised, and the battle for the truth had just begun.

As they navigate the treacherous landscape of the city, evading pursuit, they must also contend with potential betrayal within their ranks. Trust becomes a central theme as they prepare for their most daring operation yet. The next chapter should open with the group facing an unexpected internal conflict, adding another layer of suspense to their mission.

End of Chapter 3

CHAPTER 4

The Veil of Deception

In the dim light of the warehouse, the group gathered closer, the tension palpable in the air. Zara's arrival had thrown a wrench into their carefully laid plans, and distrust simmered beneath the surface.

"Explain," Rynn demanded, their voice steady but tinged with an edge of urgency.

Zara stepped forward, her eyes scanning the group. "I've been monitoring corporate communications, hacking into their secure channels. They know about the Shadow Network's backup location. It's a setup. They're planning to ambush anyone who tries to access it."

Cray frowned, processing this information. "But how did they find out? We've been careful."

"The corporations have their ways. Spies, informants, surveillance... it's a network of deceit," Zara replied. "And they're not just after the Shadow Network. They're aiming to eradicate all dissent in the city."

Eloise looked at Kai, then back at Zara. "So, what do you suggest we do? Abandon the mission?"

"No," Zara said firmly. "I suggest we turn their trap against them. We hit them where they least expect it."

The group listened intently as Zara outlined her plan. It was audacious, requiring precision and a level of coordination they hadn't attempted before. They would split into two teams – one to serve as a diversion, drawing the corporations' forces to a decoy location, while the other team infiltrated the real backup site.

As they debated the details, Kai's unease grew. "This is risky," he said, voicing the concern that hung in the air. "We're not just dealing with data theft anymore. This is direct confrontation."

Rynn considered his words, then turned to the group. "Kai is right. This escalates our fight to a new level. But we have no choice. The corporations have forced our hand."

Cray nodded, his resolve hardening. "We knew this wouldn't be easy. If we want to expose the truth, we have to be willing to fight for it."

The plan was set. Rynn and Kai would lead the diversion team, using their technical expertise to create a convincing ruse. Cray, Eloise, and Zara would infiltrate the backup site, retrieving the critical data.

As they prepared to leave, Zara pulled Cray aside. "There's something else," she said in a low voice. "I have reason to believe there's a higher power at play here, someone pulling the strings above the corporations."

Cray's eyes narrowed. "Who?"

"I don't have a name yet. But be careful. We're stepping into a larger game, and we don't know all the players."

With this ominous warning ringing in their ears, the group split up, vanishing into the night to execute their most dangerous mission yet. The chapter closed on a city that was a chessboard of power plays, with the group now active players in a game that reached far beyond the neon-lit streets.

The warehouse, once buzzing with strategy and planning, had quieted down as each team departed on their respective missions. The night enveloped the city, a shroud under which they would enact their daring plan.

Team Diversion: Rynn and Kai

Rynn and Kai, armed with an arsenal of digital tools, made their way to an abandoned tech hub on the east side of the city. The area, once a bustling center of innovation, now lay forgotten, its skeletal structures a monument to abandoned dreams.

Inside the hub, Kai set up their equipment, fingers flying over keyboards to initiate the diversion. "Activating the decoy signal in three... two... one..."

On the other side of the city, alarms blared within the corporate security offices as their systems detected a breach at the supposed backup site. Teams were dispatched, rushing towards the decoy location, falling into the trap Rynn and Kai had set.

Rynn monitored the corporations' movements, a grim satisfaction in their eyes. "Phase one is a success. They've taken the bait."

Team Infiltration: Cray, Eloise, and Zara

Meanwhile, Cray, Eloise, and Zara approached the true backup site, a nondescript building nestled in the heart of the city's industrial district. The area was eerily quiet, the hum of the city a distant echo.

Cray led the way, his device scanning for security measures. "Looks like we have multiple layers of encryption. This won't be easy," he muttered.

Eloise readied her nanobots. "Let's do what we do best." She released them, and they swarmed ahead, seeking out security weaknesses.

Zara, ever vigilant, kept watch. Her intuition, honed through years of operating in the city's underbelly, sensed something amiss. "We're not alone," she whispered.

Cray and Eloise paused, scanning their surroundings. It was then they noticed it – a faint clicking sound, almost imperceptible. Cameras.

"They're watching us," Cray said, a note of urgency in his voice. "We need to move, now."

They quickened their pace, navigating the building's labyrinthine corridors towards the heart of the data center. The nanobots worked tirelessly, disabling security protocols that stood in their way.

As they reached the data center, a sense of triumph was overshadowed by the feeling of being observed. They were in the lion's den, and the lion was very much aware of their presence.

The Twist

Just as they began to download the data, the screens around them flickered to life. A face appeared, enigmatic and cold, its eyes seeming to pierce through the digital divide.

"Welcome," the figure spoke, their voice resonating through the room with a chilling calmness. "I must commend your skills. But you are playing a dangerous game."

Cray, Eloise, and Zara exchanged tense glances. This was the higher power Zara had warned about - the puppeteer behind the corporate veil.

"Who are you?" Cray demanded, his hand still on the console, the data transfer blinking steadily.

The figure smiled, a calculated, unsettling gesture. "Let's just say, I am someone who appreciates the value of information. And you've just broken into my vault."

Eloise's eyes narrowed. "You're behind the corporations?"

"In a manner of speaking," the figure replied. "But my interests are... broader. I control much more than just corporate secrets. You've stepped into a world much larger than your Shadow Network or your little rebellion."

Zara stepped forward. "What do you want?"

The figure's gaze seemed to penetrate the screen. "I want to offer you a choice. Join me. With your skills, you could be invaluable. Or continue this futile resistance and face consequences far beyond your comprehension."

The offer hung in the air, a venomous temptation laced with danger. They were at a crossroads, the path they chose next could define the future of their struggle.

Cray, his hand steady, completed the data transfer. "We don't make deals with puppet masters," he stated firmly.

The figure chuckled, a sound that sent shivers down their spines. "Very well. But remember, you've made a powerful enemy today."

The screens went black, leaving them in near darkness, the only light coming from the blinking console indicating the successful data transfer.

They quickly gathered the drive and made their escape, the weight of the encounter heavy on their minds. As they disappeared into the night, the chapter closed, leaving a trail of questions and the palpable sense of a looming storm.

The Eye of the Storm

Back at their makeshift headquarters, a disused factory on the outskirts of the city, the group gathered, the data drive with the stolen information lying at the center of the table. The encounter with the enigmatic figure had left them shaken, the gravity of their situation hanging heavily in the air.

Eloise broke the silence. "We knew we were taking on the corporations, but this... this is something else. This person, whoever they are, is pulling strings at a level we didn't anticipate."

Cray, his eyes fixed on the data drive, replied, "We've uncovered something bigger than we thought. But it doesn't change our goal. We expose the corruption, no matter how high it goes."

Kai, still reeling from the revelation, added, "The data we've got could be the key. We need to analyze it, see what we're dealing with."

Rynn, always the strategist, interjected, "We also need to stay one step ahead. This figure, they won't take our defiance lightly. We should expect retaliation."

Zara, who had been quiet, spoke up. "There's more. I've been tracking some unusual activity in the city's surveillance network. It's like they're searching for something, or someone."

The group pondered this new piece of information. It was clear that their actions had set off a chain reaction, one that was now evolving beyond their control.

As they delved into the data, a startling discovery was made. The information did not just implicate the corporations in corruption and exploitation; it hinted at a deeper conspiracy, involving high-ranking officials in the city government and even international entities.

The room fell into a stunned silence. The scope of the conspiracy was far-reaching, threatening to upend the very fabric of their society. They were no longer just fighting corporate greed; they were up against a global syndicate of power and manipulation.

"We need to get this information out there," Eloise said, determination in her voice. "The public deserves to know."

"But we have to be smart about it," Rynn cautioned. "If we just release everything, they'll discredit it. We need undeniable proof."

The plan was forming, a complex operation that would require all their skills and resources. They would need to gather more evidence, corroborate the data, and find a way to release it that would leave no room for doubt or dismissal.

Just as they were finalizing their strategy, a new twist came in the form of an urgent message from an unknown source. The message was cryptic, but its meaning was clear: they had an ally within the syndicate, someone offering help.

The chapter closed with the group facing a new, unexpected variable. Trusting this unknown ally could be a trap, but it could also be their only chance to penetrate the depths of the conspiracy they were fighting against.

The air in the factory was thick with tension as the group grappled with the new information and the mysterious offer of assistance. The stakes were higher than ever, and the path forward was fraught with uncertainty.

"Who could this ally be?" Kai pondered aloud, re-reading the cryptic message. "And how can we be sure it's not a trap?"

Cray leaned back, his mind racing. "We can't be sure. But this might be our only shot at getting inside information. We have to take the risk, but with caution."

Eloise nodded in agreement. "Let's set up a meeting, but on our terms. Neutral ground, and we stay hidden until we're sure it's safe."

The plan was risky, but it was the best course of action under the circumstances. They decided to send a coded response, arranging a meeting at an abandoned subway station, long forgotten by the city's inhabitants.

Meanwhile, Rynn and Zara focused on analyzing the data they had extracted. The layers of information were complex, a web of transactions, communications, and covert operations that spanned the globe.

As they dug deeper, a pattern began to emerge. The syndicate was not just involved in economic manipulation; they were influencing political events, destabilizing regions for their gain, and even orchestrating conflicts. The depth of the corruption was staggering.

"This goes beyond corruption. It's like they're playing god, shaping the world to their design," Zara said, aghast at the revelations.

"We need to expose them, now more than ever," Rynn declared, their voice firm. "But we have to be smart. We can't let this information get buried or twisted."

The team worked through the night, piecing together a plan to disseminate the information in a way that would make the biggest impact. They decided to create a series of data dumps, each timed to coincide with major news cycles, and to distribute them through various channels to ensure widespread dissemination.

As dawn broke, casting a pale light through the grimy windows of the factory, the group prepared to meet their mysterious ally. Tensions were high as they arrived at the abandoned subway station, a place that time had forgotten, its walls echoing with the ghosts of a bustling past.

Cray, Eloise, and Kai took positions, hidden in the shadows, while Rynn waited in the open, a silent beacon in the desolate station. Minutes stretched into hours as they waited, the silence oppressive.

Then, a figure emerged from the tunnel's darkness, their steps cautious but deliberate. As they stepped into the dim light, their identity sent a shockwave through the team.

Standing before them was not a stranger, but a familiar face, one they had encountered before in their fight against the corporations. It was...

End of Chapter 5

CHAPTER 6

Unseen Alliances

The abandoned subway station, once a symbol of the city's progress, now stood as a witness to a pivotal moment. The figure emerging from the shadows was none other than Lena, a high-ranking official in the city government, previously thought to be aligned with the corporations.

The group's initial shock quickly turned to suspicion. Lena, with her impeccable suit and composed demeanor, seemed out of place in the desolate subway station.

"Why should we trust you?" Cray asked, his voice echoing in the cavernous space. "Last we knew, you were in the corporations' pocket."

Lena held up her hand, a plea for a chance to explain. "I understand your distrust. But I assure you, my intentions are aligned with yours. I've seen the corruption from the inside, and I can't stand by any longer."

Eloise, skeptical, narrowed her eyes. "And we're just supposed to take your word for it?"

Lena sighed, a hint of weariness in her eyes. "I have information. Information that can bring them down. But I need your help to make it public. They're watching my every move."

The revelation of Lena's defection and her offer of inside information forced the group to reconsider their strategy. An ally within the city's power structure could be invaluable, but the risk of betrayal was high.

As they deliberated, an urgent message from Zara disrupted their meeting. "The network is under attack. It's a coordinated strike, they're trying to take us down."

The news of the strike against the Shadow Network was a stark reminder of the danger they were in. Time was running out, and their enemies were closing in.

"We need to act now," Rynn declared, turning to Lena. "If your information is as valuable as you say, we use it. We hit them before they can regroup."

With a new sense of urgency, the group formed a plan. Lena would provide the critical information, which they would combine with the data they had already gathered. The objective was clear: expose the syndicate's activities and bring the fight to the public eye.

As they prepared to leave, a sudden rumble echoed through the subway station, followed by the sound of approaching footsteps. They were not alone.

Cray signaled the group to take cover. Shadows moved in the darkness, the glint of weapons barely visible. They were surrounded, the enemy having tracked them down to their clandestine meeting.

The chapter closed with the group braced for a confrontation, their plans hanging in the balance. The battle for the truth had reached a critical juncture, and the next moments would define the future of their resistance.

End of Chapter 6

CHAPTER 7

The Tides of Conflict

In the dimly lit subway station, the sound of encroaching footsteps grew louder, echoing off the walls. The group, hidden in the shadows, prepared for the inevitable confrontation. Cray signaled to the others, his eyes sharp and focused.

"We need to avoid a direct fight if we can," he whispered. "Let's move towards the east tunnel. There's an old maintenance hatch there. We might be able to slip out."

The group began to stealthily maneuver towards the hatch, their movements a silent dance in the darkness. Lena, despite her usual composure in the halls of power, seemed tense, her eyes darting around nervously.

Eloise, leading the way, paused suddenly, signaling for silence. A shadow detached itself from the darkness ahead, moving directly towards them. Without hesitation, Eloise deployed her nanobots, which swirled around the figure, disorienting them long enough for Kai to knock them out silently.

As they reached the hatch, a burst of light flooded the tunnel, followed by the sound of armed agents pouring in. The group realized escape was no longer an option. It was time to stand their ground.

What ensued was a frenzied skirmish, a test of their resolve and skills. Cray and Rynn fought back-to-back, their movements synchronized. Zara, using her hacking tools, disrupted the agents' communication, sowing confusion among their ranks.

Kai and Eloise worked together, using a combination of tech and ingenuity to create makeshift barriers and diversions. Lena, surprisingly adept in the heat of the moment, provided critical cover, her knowledge of tactical strategies proving invaluable.

In the midst of the chaos, a sudden explosion rocked the station, creating a momentary pause in the fighting. From the smoke emerged a group of figures, their identities obscured by the haze. As they stepped forward, the group realized they were not enemies, but members of the Shadow Network, come to their aid.

The tide of the battle shifted. With the reinforcements, the group was able to overpower the agents, turning the tables on their attackers. As the last of the agents retreated, the group took a moment to catch their breath, the adrenaline of the skirmish still coursing through their veins.

The leader of the Shadow Network reinforcements, a grizzled veteran of the city's underground struggles, approached them. "We've been monitoring the situation. Knew you'd run into trouble," he said, his voice rough but reassuring. "Seems like you've stirred up quite the hornet's nest."

Cray, still catching his breath, nodded in gratitude. "Thanks for the assist. We wouldn't have made it without you."

The veteran nodded. "The fight's just beginning. What you've uncovered, it's bigger than any of us imagined. The whole city needs to know. And we're going to help you tell them."

The group gathered around, the weight of their responsibility settling in. They had allies, and together, they could make a stand. The data they had gathered, combined with Lena's insider information, painted a damning picture of corruption and manipulation that reached to the highest levels.

Eloise spoke up, determination in her voice. "We need to broadcast this, far and wide. Every screen in the city should show the truth."

The plan was audacious, requiring them to hack into the city's central broadcasting system - a feat that was risky but necessary. They would distribute the evidence in a synchronized data dump, ensuring maximum exposure.

As they prepared to leave the subway station, a new sense of purpose united them. They were no longer just a group of rebels and outcasts; they were the voice of a city crying for justice.

But as they stepped out into the early morning light, a new challenge awaited them. The city was eerily quiet, a stark contrast to the usual hum of activity. Screens across the city flickered to life, displaying a message from the enigmatic figure they had encountered before.

"I admire your persistence," the figure's voice echoed through the streets. "But you are playing a dangerous game. This is your last warning. Stand down, or face consequences beyond your comprehension."

The chapter closed with the group standing together, resolute in the face of this new threat. They had a choice to make - back down and live in the shadows, or stand up and fight for the truth.

End of Chapter 7

CHAPTER 8

The Dawn of Truth

The early morning streets of the city were unusually silent, a stark canvas awaiting the brushstrokes of revolution. The group, now more than just a band of rebels, prepared for what could be their final stand.

In an abandoned broadcast station, they set their plan into motion. Kai and Zara worked feverishly on the terminals, bypassing security protocols to gain access to the city's central broadcasting system. Eloise's nanobots swarmed over the hardware, creating a direct link for their data transmission.

Cray, Rynn, and Lena oversaw the operation, ensuring the perimeter was secure. The air was thick with tension, each second ticking by amplifying the gravity of what they were about to do.

As the sun began to rise, casting a pale golden hue over the city, the screens across the metropolis flickered to life. The group's broadcast began, a flood of data, documents, and recordings exposing the syndicate's corruption, the corporate manipulations, and the government's complicity.

The city awoke to the truth in a crescendo of realization. People gathered in the streets, their eyes fixed on the screens, their expressions a mix of shock, anger, and awakening.

Meanwhile, at the heart of the city, in a sleek tower that pierced the sky, the enigmatic figure watched the broadcast, their expression unreadable. Around them, screens displayed the unfolding chaos, the narrative they had so meticulously crafted unraveling before their eyes.

They turned to their aides, their voice calm yet laced with menace. "Shut it down. Now."

Back at the broadcast station, the group sensed the approaching storm. Armored vehicles and tactical teams advanced on their location, a physical manifestation of the syndicate's desperation.

Cray looked at his comrades, a silent question in his eyes. Lena stepped forward, her resolve clear. "We knew it might come to this. We stand our ground."

The clash was inevitable. As the forces stormed the building, the group fought with a ferocity born of conviction. Eloise's nanobots created a labyrinth of barriers, Kai jammed the attackers' communications, and Rynn provided strategic cover fire.

Zara, her fingers a blur on the keyboard, worked to keep the broadcast live. "We're still on air," she shouted over the chaos. "The whole city is watching."

Outside, the public's murmurs grew into a roar of support. Crowds began to gather, their numbers swelling, standing in solidarity with the truth they were witnessing.

In the midst of the battle, the enigmatic figure appeared, their presence commanding and ominous. "Enough!" they bellowed, and a hush fell over the skirmish.

Cray stepped forward, bruised but unbroken. "It's over. The truth is out there. You can't control it anymore."

The figure's gaze swept over the group and the screens still broadcasting to the city. A moment of realization crossed their face, a crack in their composed facade. "You think you've won," they said, a tinge of defeat in their voice. "But the truth is a double-edged sword. It can liberate, but it can also destroy."

The standoff continued, a tense silence enveloping the space. Then, unexpectedly, the figure turned and walked away, their retreat a silent concession of their defeat. The forces, now leaderless, hesitated before withdrawing, leaving the group standing amid the remnants of the battle.

As the broadcast came to an end, the group emerged from the station. The city around them had transformed. People flooded the streets, their voices rising in a chorus of newfound empowerment. The revelation of the truth had ignited a spark, the start of a profound change in the societal landscape.

Eloise, looking around at the sea of faces, felt a swell of hope. "We did it," she whispered. "We actually did it."

Kai, bandaging a wound on his arm, grinned. "We started a revolution."

Rynn, surveying the scene, nodded in agreement. "A revolution of truth. But this is just the beginning. The real work starts now."

Lena, standing beside Cray, added, "The city will need new leaders, ones who understand the value of transparency and integrity."

Cray, his gaze on the horizon, knew their journey had reached its end, but a new chapter for the city was just beginning. "Let's build a better future," he said, a sense of determination in his voice.

The group disbanded, melting back into the city that was now awakening to a new dawn. They were no longer just rebels fighting in the shadows; they were catalysts for a brighter future.

As the sun rose higher, casting its light on the streets filled with people, the chapter closed on a city reborn. The truth had set them free, and in its light, they would forge a new path.

Epilogue
In the days that followed, the city underwent profound changes. The syndicate's grip on power was broken, and new leaders

emerged, guided by the principles of transparency and fairness. The group's members, once outcasts and rebels, now played integral roles in rebuilding the society they had fought to change.

Their story became a beacon, a testament to the power of truth and the strength of the human spirit. And though they each walked their own paths, the bonds they forged in the fight for justice remained, a lasting legacy of their struggle and triumph.

The End